D1536179

ALPHABET PUZZLE

For Eileen and Lin

Copyright © 1988 by Jill Downie
First published in Great Britain by Andersen Press Ltd
All rights reserved. No part of this book may be reproduced or utilized in any form or by any means, electronic or mechanical, including photocopying, recording or by any information storage and retrieval system, without permission in writing from the Publisher. Inquiries should be addressed to Lothrop, Lee & Shepard Books, a division of William Morrow & Company, Inc., 105 Madison Avenue, New York, New York 10016. Printed in Great Britain
First U.S. Edition 1 2 3 4 5 6 7 8 9 10

Library of Congress Number 88-80278

ALPHABET

PUZZLE

?

~ Jill Downie ~

Lothrop, Lee & Shepard Books
New York

A, a

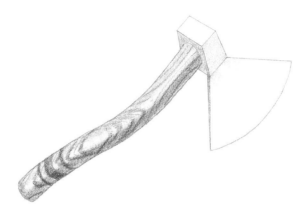

is for
axe

B,b

is for

?

B, b

is for

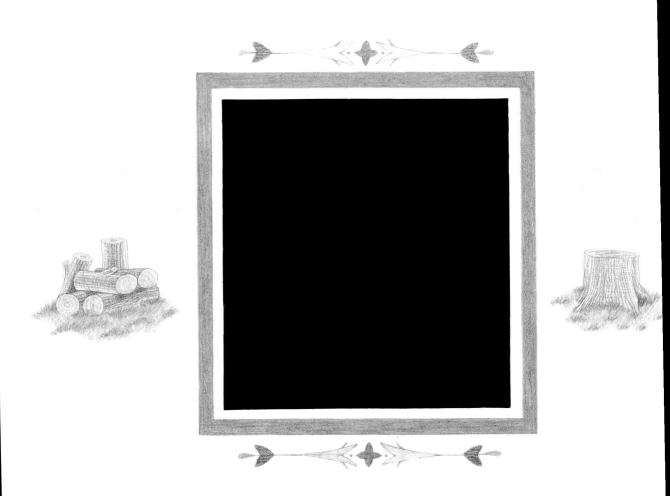

bark

C, c

is for

camel

D is for

is for

?

desert

E,e

is for

egg

F, f

is for

?

frying-pan

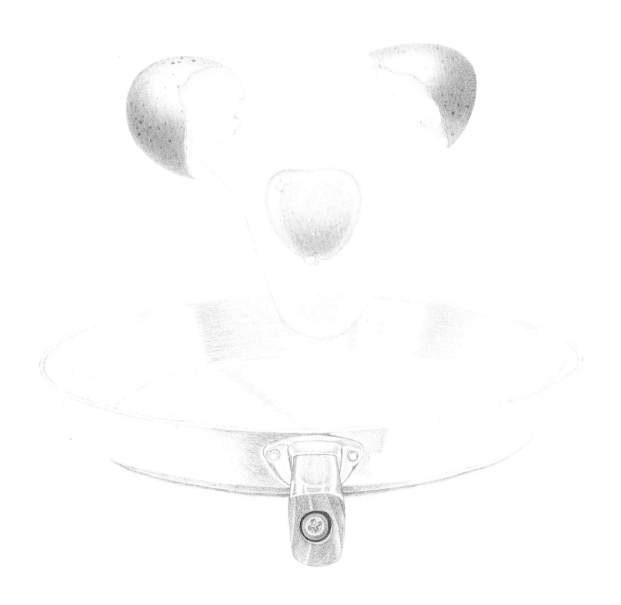

G, g

is for

garland

H,h

is for

?

hat

I, i

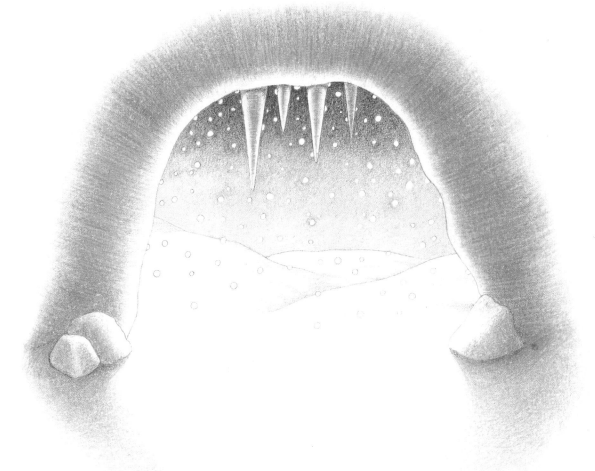

is for
icicles

J, j

is for

?

jaws

K, k

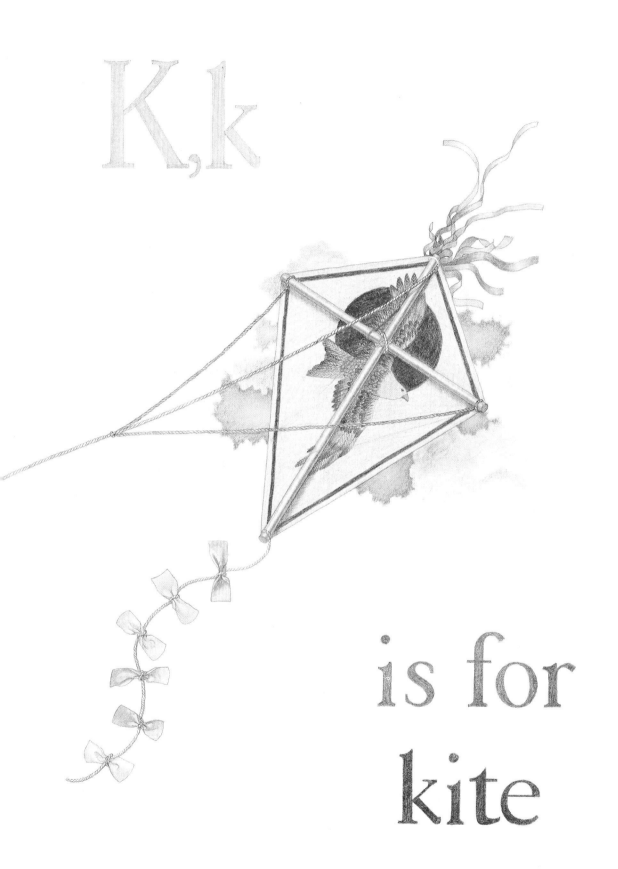

is for
kite

L, l

is for

?

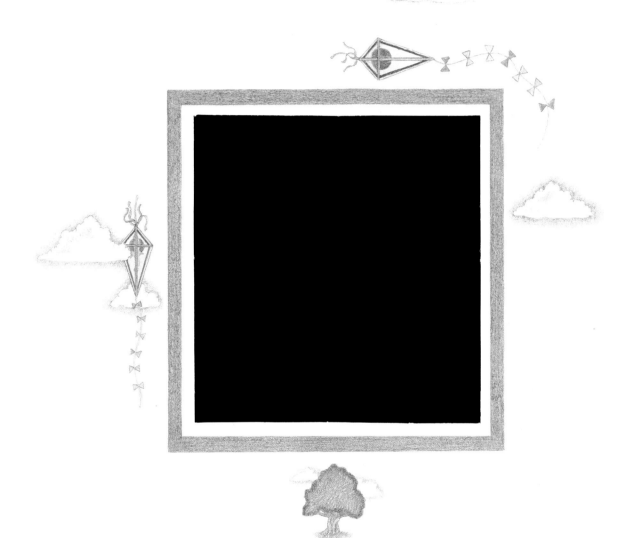

ladder

M,m

is for

moon

N,n

is for

?

nightingale

O, o

is for

oven

P, p

is for

?

picnic

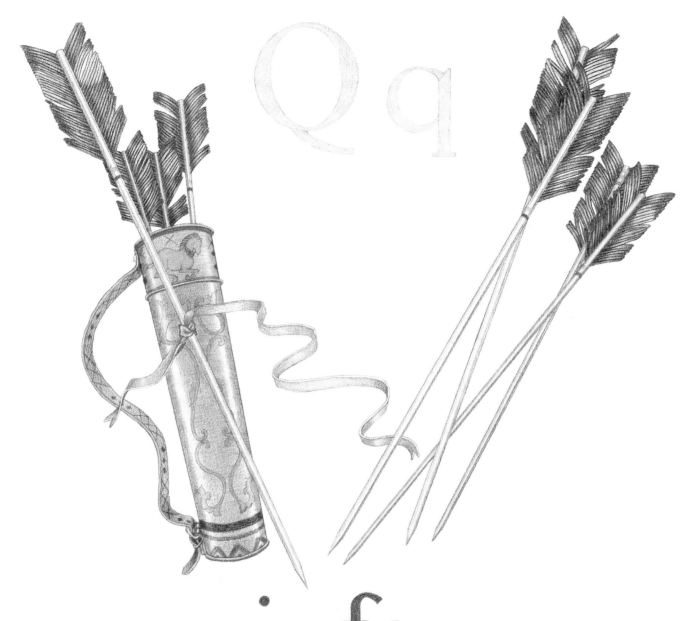

Qq

is for
quiver

R,r

is for

?

reeds

S,s

is for
shoes

T, t

is for

?

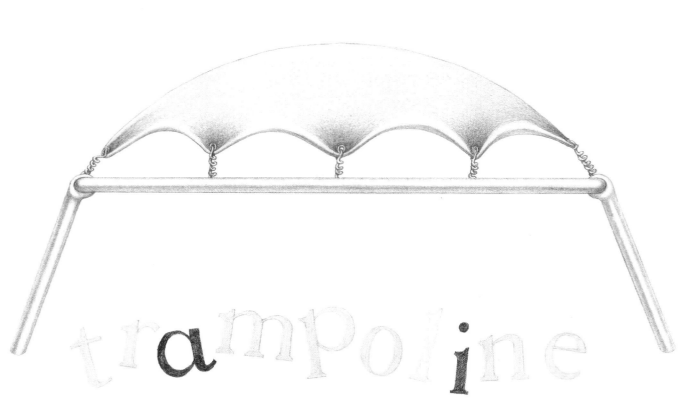

trampoline

U,u

is for

umbrella

V, v

is for

?

vase

W, w

is for

waves

X, x

is for

?

x-ray fish

Y,y

is for

yak

Z, z

is for

?

zig-zag